# JOSHUA'S WESTWARD JOURNAL

## BY JOAN ANDERSON
## PHOTOGRAPHS BY GEORGE ANCONA

William Morrow and Company, Inc. / New York

## ACKNOWLEDGMENTS

Doing a historical photo essay, especially when it involves a move west and two major locations, takes detailed planning, generous support, and a back-up crew from myriad sources.

At the Conner Prairie Pioneer Settlement in Noblesville, Indiana, we wish to thank John Patterson, who planned and scouted out appropriate locations for photographs; Bonnie Carter, who not only helped with props, sets, and makeup, but also provided shelter, coffee, and support for weary actors and authors; and our stalwart family—Sam Dodson (Pa), Stephanie Cochran (Ma), P. J. Rutar (Joshua), Myra Church (Becky), and Sue Cane (Cousin Verna)—who worked ten-hour days to help us show the life of a pioneer family.

From the Living History Farms in Des Moines, Iowa, where much of our story was shot, we are most grateful to Tom Morain, who directed us to the appropriate literature, helped us work out a complicated but historically accurate storyline, and housed us most graciously in Living History Farms' Solar House; David Miles, who allowed us to pick his brains about the homesteading era; and to all the Living History Farms interpreters, particularly Darwin Thede.

Finally, we thank Andrea Curley, whose support, honest criticism, and original thinking gave this book a personal and poignant tone.

Joan Anderson          George Ancona

*To P. J. Rutar—J. A. · To Bob Moore—G. A.*

*Library of Congress Cataloging-in-Publication Data*
*Anderson, Joan.*
*Joshua's westward journal.*
*Summary: In 1836, Joshua and his family travel as pioneers into Illinois, where they survive disastrous hardships to establish a prosperous farm of their own.*
*[1. Frontier and pioneer life–Illinois–Fiction.  2. Illinois–Fiction]*
*I. Ancona, George, ill.  II. Title.*
*PZ7.A5367Jo  1987  [Fic]  87-5509*
*ISBN 0-688-06680-1*
*ISBN 0-688-06681-X (lib. bdg.)*

A half million Americans streamed west in the mid-1800s. They were called emigrants because they were headed for territories that had not yet become states.

These brave people, with hope for new opportunities and prosperity spurring them on, usually set out in late spring, timing their departure to coincide with nature: They needed the prairie grasses for their animals to feed on along the route, and they had to arrive at their destination in time to build shelters and plant crops.

Today we don't think much when we hop in our cars with only a map, duffel bag, and a cooler of snacks, knowing full well that motels, gas stations, and towns wait to serve us.

Imagine the same journey in an overloaded, narrow, horse- or oxen-drawn wagon. Every inch of space was filled either with belongings the pioneers couldn't bear to leave behind or necessities needed for homesteading. Enough food, feed, water, and supplies also had to be aboard to sustain a family over empty stretches of wilderness. Stagecoach stops, small towns, and farmhouses were rare. These pioneers were the first wave that would eventually open up the territory for others to follow behind.

Who were these people eager to leave established homes and travel west? Many were like the fictional Samuel Carpenter, who had been infected by the "Iowa fever." The *Iowa News* proclaimed that the prairie was paradise: "It is seldom that a person who has resided out here can ever content himself to return east."

Words such as these made the Carpenter family leave Pennsylvania and head for the government-built trail, called the National Road. We accompany Samuel and Martha Carpenter, and their children, Joshua and Becky, meeting up with them as they leave Indianapolis, and follow their journey into the wilderness as they face all the challenges of pioneer life.

*July 7, 1836: I'm beginning to understand what it means to be a pioneer. There's no turning back now.*

**J**oshua recorded his thoughts in the journal he was keeping as the Carpenters moved west. Gazing out the back of the wagon, he saw nothing but two long lines of wheel tracks and eighteen-inch tree stumps down the middle of the endless, dusty road. There were no signs of other emigrants, either following behind or up ahead. Just as well, Joshua figured, as the road was only wide enough for one wagon. It was rare even to find a spot big enough to pull over and impossible to turn the wagon around if they should consider returning to civilization.

Being so alone and away from everything, Joshua began to realize just how much the four of them would have to depend on each other. He had to admit that he did feel somewhat secure surrounded by all their belongings, and he was excited about their rather uncertain future. What territory would they finally settle in, he wondered, Iowa or Illinois? And what would the land look like? These questions kept his mind racing when there wasn't anything else to do.

*July 10: Pa promised that our journey would be an adventure. I won't admit to him that staring at an endless road and doing trail chores is not exactly my idea of an adventure.*

Pa's hope was that the family would be able to cover fifteen or twenty miles a day. "It's important," he said, "if we hope to reach our destination with time to spare before winter sets in."

And so all four Carpenters pitched in as they traveled and when they camped.

Ma kept the wagon organized and clean. After all, for the time being it was their home, even if it was on wheels. Pa tended to the wagon and cared for Henry and Jack, the Carpenters' horses. He would grease the wheel hubs, check the harnesses, and look out for trouble. It was Becky's and Joshua's job to walk alongside or run up ahead and warn Pa of big holes or large rocks embedded in the hardened surface. They had already broken the axle back in Ohio and didn't want to lose more time with a similar accident.

Some days were harder than others. And passing frequent gravestones that indicated fellow emigrants who hadn't survived the harsh trail life didn't exactly lift Joshua's spirits. Each day he hoped something fun or dangerous or unusual would occur just to break the monotony.

Walking was fun when it wasn't too hot and there were other travelers to talk to. But the conditions on the National Road were such that Becky's and Joshua's shoes filled with pebbles and dirt, creating painful blisters all over the bottoms of their feet. Whenever they stopped, Pa had to apply a plaster to their aching soles so they could continue on.

*July 12: Finally some company! We met up with a few wagons and made camp together.*

Pa had told Joshua that lots of folks were moving west, but until now the Carpenters hadn't met up with too many others. Becky claimed that she hadn't counted more than ten wagons since they left Indianapolis.

As they settled in for their first real camp meeting, pulling their wagon up close to the others, Joshua learned that these were three families traveling together. He wished Pa had been able to persuade the Bakers and the Kreugers back home to join them, but neither family had the "Iowa fever" as Pa did.

Joshua and Becky watched as the men set up a huge tent. Apparently, these folks had pooled their resources, each wagon carrying different supplies, so they could share not only the warmth of each other's company, but tools, food, and shelter, too.

The women scurried about, borrowing from each other to prepare the meal, and Ma got right into the spirit of things as if she'd known them all her life.

Soon Joshua and Becky could smell meat cooking and biscuits baking. The aromas kept them close to the crackling fire, their plates in hand, waiting for the first portions to be served. After supper everyone sang and passed news. It seemed as if they had created a little town in the wilderness.

Later that evening, Joshua reluctantly retired to his tick. As he lay on the ground staring at the stars that filled the endless sky, he felt sad about what would happen in the morning: the families climbing back into their wagons, heading off in different directions, all of them in search of their dreams.

*July 14: We have to find water soon. The barrel's plumb near empty.*

It had been five days since the Carpenters had been able to fill their water barrel. And because of the intense heat, all of them, Henry and Jack included, had quenched their thirst more than usual.

"Joshua," Pa called, concern in his voice, "check *The Immigrant Guide*. Do you see any mention of a creek or stage stop nearby?"

The guidebook had proved useless since they had left Indianapolis. Most of the stages it mentioned had closed down, and with the drought the creeks were pretty dry. Nevertheless Joshua looked. "There's supposed to be a stream off the road a piece," he answered.

The Carpenters listened and watched. Sure enough, not more than an hour later they all heard the unmistakable sound of rushing water above the clopping of the horses' hoofs.

"Samuel," Ma exclaimed as they drew up near the stream, "this is such a good spot, why don't we stay for the night? While you menfolk clean up, I can wash and dry the laundry right here along the banks. That way we can start off fresh and clean tomorrow."

Pa's expression told Becky and Joshua that Ma's plan was fine. In no time Joshua had torn off his clothes and was jumping into the water. When he came up for air, Pa was beside him, soaping up his broad chest.

"I never thought a river could make me so happy," Joshua remarked. "But since we left home all my ideas are changing."

"I told you we were in for an adventure, son," Pa said with a knowing smile. And with that the two Carpenter men dove under and raced to the other side.

*July 19: Hurray. Meat tonight!*

Finding the stream seemed to change the Carpenters' luck as far as their water supply was concerned. It rained steadily for the next few days. First they had no water and then too much, Joshua thought miserably as he huddled in the corner of the wagon to keep dry and warm. And because of all the rain, they were unable to get a fire started and have a real supper.

Some days during this rainy spell, they barely made six miles as Henry and Jack kept stalling in mud holes. Ma seemed to sense her family's sour mood and was determined to perk up their spirits. While Becky and Joshua helped get the horses going again, Joshua noticed that his mother would wander off, talking to other travelers.

When they spotted their first farmhouse, Ma insisted they stop in the hope of buying some fresh meat. She returned clutching a heavy burlap bag. As she climbed up to her seat, she announced, "Samuel, you'd best find us a decent place to camp, y'hear? We are going to have us a feast!"

Becky's stomach growled in anticipation as Joshua and Pa began to look for a place. When

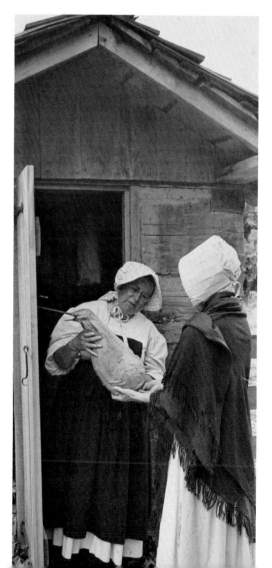

they found it, Ma sent the family off to do chores while she prepared her surprise. As the delicious smells drifted through the air, the family began to gather around the wagon. Ma took great delight in watching their reactions. She had covered their kitchen table with a tablecloth, set it with some fancy plates, and piled it high with fixin's. There were baked ham, scalloped potatoes, fresh bread, and even a cake for dessert.

How the Carpenters enjoyed their feast in the middle of the prairie!

After their stomachs were full, Ma said cheerfully, "Becky and Joshua, you two have been working so hard I'll not have you cleaning up tonight. Go off and have yourselves some fun. But don't wander too far, y'hear?"

The two children gladly complied with their mother's order.

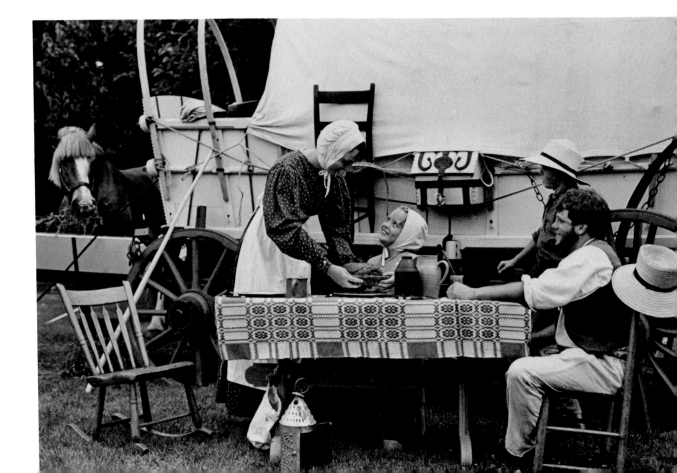

But the tranquil evening soon came to an end. Becky and Joshua hadn't gone far when a shrill scream pierced the air. "Help! Help! Come quick."

"That sounds like Ma," Joshua said, grabbing Becky by the hand and racing back toward the campsite.

They found Ma sprawled on the ground, the big iron kettle tipped over beside her leg. One look and Joshua knew she had scalded herself badly. "Becky, tend to Ma while I fetch Pa," Joshua ordered his sister.

By the time he returned with his father, Becky had already pulled out the medicine kit. Pa knelt down to dress the wound, covering half of Ma's leg with ointment and bandages. "Help me move her into the wagon," he said curtly. It scared Joshua to see his father so worried.

"Now no more fussin', y'hear?" Ma muttered as Pa tucked her in.

That night Joshua tossed and turned, wanting to believe that Ma's brave front meant she'd be all right. But he couldn't stop worrying at the severity of her burn.

*July 22: I'm scared. Ma's not getting any better, and to make matters worse she's developed a fever.*

Pa decided that it would be unwise to continue traveling until Ma's leg had started to heal. But after three days of trying various teas and other remedies, she still showed no signs of gaining strength, and Pa thought it best to push on.

"We must try and get to my kinfolk in western Illinois," Pa confided to Joshua. "Ma needs a doctor," he continued. "The fever she's developed is a sure sign of infection. I've checked the map. I reckon Springfield's our best bet for finding a doctor."

"Springfield!" Joshua gasped. "That's days away!"

"I know," Pa whispered, "but if we travel day and night, I figure we could be there in three days."

"You and I can take turns at the reins, and Becky can tend to Ma," Joshua suggested, eager to do anything to help.

They pushed on, and Henry and Jack, sensing the urgency, quickened their pace each night. Pa hardly said a word. His mind was only on Ma, who lay much too quietly in the back.

By the third night they were so exhausted that Pa finally called a halt to their frantic pace. "We'll camp here and hopefully reach Springfield by noon tomorrow," he said wearily.

Becky made a fire, but when she heard the howling of the prairie wolves, she asked Pa to build it up a little higher. "Could we all sleep together by the campfire?" she asked.

Pa had just set up her little tent. "I think you'd be more comfortable under shelter, Becky," he said.

Just then Ma's weakened voice called from the wagon, "Samuel, maybe if you told the children a story they'd quiet down."

"All right," he agreed, "come gather round." He seemed relieved to get his wife's guidance.

Joshua listened hard, hoping the story would take his mind off Ma, but it didn't. He kept thinking about the pact that he and his father had made before leaving home. Together, the Carpenter men would protect the womenfolk. All of a sudden that promise seemed impossible.

The sun was just coming up when Joshua stirred. The unmistakable sound of dirt being shoveled had woken him. He was so tired, though, that he turned over and dozed off again. When his eyes blinked open for the second time, he heard a quiet sobbing. Joshua bolted upright and pulled back the tent flap. There, sitting on the back of the wagon, was Pa, his head buried in his hands.

"Pa," Joshua wailed as he ran toward his father. He saw a mound of dirt out of the corner of his eye but didn't want to accept what he knew must be true.

"Tell me it's not Ma," he begged, flinging himself at his father.

"I'm sorry, son," Pa mumbled.

"No, Pa, no!" Joshua cried. "She was feeling a little better last night. I just *knew* she was ... and we're almost to Springfield."

"I know, I know," Pa said again and again, "but when I took her some tea this morning she didn't wake up. The good Lord has spared her from any more suffering, Joshua."

Just then Pa looked up and saw Becky standing at the entrance of her tent. Wordlessly he held out his arms and she rushed to him. The three of them held each other tightly for a long time.

"We've got to bury her proper," Pa said finally, regaining his composure. "Now go off and pick some flowers for Ma. She'd like that, I know."

Joshua and Becky obeyed, and they returned in a bit, their arms laden with every color of wild flower the prairie had to offer.

"Now then, place them by the marker," Pa instructed gently as he began to thumb through the Bible. As Joshua knelt down, he froze. Pa had placed a marker that said *Martha Carpenter, 1808–1836*. It looked just like all the other markers he had seen along the trail—only this one . . . this one belonged to his ma.

"Stand by me," Pa said, motioning the children into place nearby. "I shall read the Twenty-third Psalm." He began, "The Lord is my shepherd, I shall not want. . . ."

Joshua had trouble concentrating. He knew this verse was read at funerals. He'd heard it back home, but it had never meant much to him until now. This couldn't be happening, he said over and over again to himself, until Pa interrupted his thoughts and asked if he would like to say something.

Anger surged through Joshua's body. How could Pa ask such a thing? And then he caught himself, realizing that his father was only trying to do the right thing.

Joshua thought for a moment. "Good-bye, Ma," he mumbled. Then Pa said, "Amen," and it was over. Joshua ran off behind their wagon and wept bitterly.

The next thing he felt was a big arm around his shoulder. "Come on now, son," Pa said, "we've got to be moving on."

"And leave Ma?" Joshua asked incredulously.

Pa nodded and led his grief-stricken son up to the wagon seat. It felt strange to be leaving Ma so soon, but Joshua knew they had no choice. Her spirit, even some of her words, would be traveling with them. Ma was always the optimist, making the best of bad situations, and she would certainly want Joshua to do the same now. Besides, it was important to take care of Pa, he thought.

Joshua straightened up in his seat and gazed out over the prairie. The grassy meadows looked like one huge garden—pink verbena, bluebells, wild indigo. Joshua could picture Ma and Becky picking bunches to fancy up the wagon. The sweet-smelling fields and bright sky lifted his spirits enough that the rest of the day's journey flew by.

As the sun began to set, they noticed quite a bit of activity up ahead. "Look, Pa," Joshua said, pointing to a small wooden sign, "the Oak Grove Stage Stop!"

"That's my uncle's place, all right," Pa remarked, sounding relieved. They turned off the main road and rambled down a heavily wooded path. "There it is!" Becky exclaimed, pointing to a huge, rectangular log building that boasted a porch all the way around. There were signs indicating a store, inn, and post office.

As soon as the horses came to a halt, Pa hopped off the wagon and shouted, "Uncle Isaac, you there?"

A strong-looking man, about fifty, came bounding out. "That you, Samuel?" he bellowed, moving quickly to grab Pa's hand. "Well land sakes, it's good to see ya. Ida, Verna, look who's here," he called to his wife and niece. Just as the children rushed onto the porch, Uncle Isaac asked, "Where's Martha?" A heavy silence fell over the family as Pa broke the news.

"Oh, no," Aunt Ida gasped, covering her mouth in disbelief. "Come inside," she beckoned, " and let us make you comfortable."

"That's just what Ma would have said," Joshua thought as they were swept inside.

"Verna fixes a big supper every day for all the travelers passin' through," Uncle Isaac explained as he cleared a place for the Carpenters at a long wooden table. "You're just in time to eat. Now then," he said, motioning for Pa to sit, "tell us what happened."

While Pa talked, Joshua and Becky feasted on monkey bread, cabbage slaw, trout, wheat rolls, and blackberry pie, all of them treats they had missed during the long wagon ride.

When Pa finished, Uncle Isaac broached the obvious: "Have you considered how you'll manage without Martha, Samuel?" As every emigrant knew, women were essential, not just to tend to the house and children but to help with the farming as well.

Pa said nothing, his eyes brimming with tears.

"You can't go much farther, what with the youngins," Aunt Ida said as she gently patted Pa's hand. "Won't you stay here a bit?"

"I'm much obliged," Pa answered, "but we came all this way to make a new life. Martha would want us to start right in, and that's what we should do."

"Well, I can understand, Samuel," Uncle Isaac said sympathetically, "and as a matter of fact I think I might have just the thing ."

He grabbed a map off the sideboard and pointed to a plot of land. "See here, there's a small farm for sale not twenty miles away. A man by the name of Benedict is tending the place. Property like this will be snatched up right quick. Are ya up for seeing it as soon as tomorrow?"

"Becky can stay with us," Verna offered.

It seemed all but decided by bedtime. Joshua and Pa would mount Henry in the morning and go take a look.

They rose at sunrise and began yet another journey, riding slowly through the heavily wooded trail, neither of them saying much. They were two men alone, attempting to make something out of a sad situation. No matter what they laid claim to, would it ever seem like home without Ma, Joshua wondered, as he held on to Pa tighter than usual.

They located the two cabins and the fork in the creek, all the landmarks Uncle Isaac had told them to look for. "When you come to a clearing," he had said, "you'll find the farm."

*July 27: And suddenly there it was . . . down in a valley . . . one of the most perfect little farms anyone could imagine.*

Joshua and Pa stared, almost in disbelief. The farm seemed to have everything—not only a cabin and barn but some pens and a smoke-house, too.

"Do you think that's it?" Joshua whispered, almost afraid someone might hear him and snatch the place away.

"Looks like it to me, son. C'mon, let's see if anyone is around!" Pa gave Henry a nudge and they galloped down the hill, stopping where they spotted a man harnessing a pair of oxen.

"Would you be George Benedict?" Pa inquired.

"That's me," the man answered, reaching up to shake Pa's hand.

"I'm Samuel Carpenter. This here's my son, Joshua. We hear your farm is for sale. That so?"

"Sure is. I took it over when the Belknaps left. Can't let a good crop go fallow, not when it's so near harvest."

"How come they left?" Pa asked.

"They inherited a fancy place back east and left in a hurry. Just as well. They weren't much cut out for pioneering."

"And you, why don't you take it?"

"Still a bachelor," Mr. Benedict answered. "A man can't survive year round without a missus, y'know. So till I find me one, I'm bid-ing my time, buying up parcels of land, mak-ing something out of them, and then turning them over for a profit."

"How much are ya askin'?" Pa finally inquired.

"I reckon around eight dollars an acre," he replied. " 'Course, whoever buys it has to share the crop with me."

"Why sure," Pa agreed. "Can we look around?"

"Help yourself," Mr. Benedict said.

As they walked through the fields and examined the buildings, it was obvious that they could not pass up such an opportunity— that is, if they could afford it. "Pa," Joshua whispered, "can we pay what he's askin'?"

"I reckon we can just about manage it," Pa said after doing a bit of mental calculation.

The two Carpenters headed back to George Benedict to propose the offer. "My son and I would be mighty happy to lay claim to this place," Pa said emphatically.

"Well, would ya now," Mr. Benedict replied, a broad grin covering his face. "Welcome to Illinois, then," he ended, extending his hand. "It'll be good having extra help to bring in the harvest."

*August 3: It felt good to be digging into the land again, instead of just traveling over it.*

For the next week the three men labored from dawn to dusk readying the place so it would be fit to live in. From the looks of things, the Belknaps didn't know how to tend a farm properly. There were fences to be mended, rocks to be carted off, wheat fields that needed flailing, and tools to be made.

As Pa worked the new land, the sweat dripped off his body. Joshua sensed that with each passing day his father was gaining more strength. He didn't seem sad and preoccupied anymore. Perhaps it was because Pa was getting on with the dream that all four Carpenters had shared.

*August 5: Exactly nine weeks after leaving Pennsylvania, we went back to Oak Grove to collect Becky and bring her home.*

It felt strange to be in the wagon again, surrounded by all their belongings, but Joshua felt good that Cousin Verna had offered to stay with them until they were properly settled in. As Joshua looked at her thinly lined face, he realized that her life had been hard, too. Pa had told him that she came west after her intended died of the cholera. She needed to make a new life for herself, he said, and with the prairie opening up like it was, there was more than enough woman's work to be done.

As they continued to bump along, Joshua's eyes rested upon Becky. "Y'know, I missed you, Becky," he found himself saying.

"You did?" his sister replied, hardly believing her ears. Joshua rarely complimented her.

"Well, I'm not so sure she had time to miss you," Cousin Verna added jokingly. "Becky here has been minding the store and tending the inn. You know, Samuel, she is one helpful young lady. Once she got started there was no stopping her."

"That's my Becky," Pa shouted back. "She's a worker, just like her ma."

There was an awkward pause—something Joshua had grown to despise. At the very mention of Ma everyone went quiet. "Well, not this time," he thought. "This is an important day in our family, and if Ma were here she wouldn't let anything spoil it."

"Wait till you see our place, Becky!" he interjected quickly. "We have chickens and a smokehouse and a cozy loft to sleep in, and acres and acres of land."

"Is it so, Pa?" Becky asked, unbelieving.

"You'll find out for yourself," Pa answered. Soon they came to the now familiar clearing, and Pa halted the horses. "Well, there it is," he announced, gesturing grandly.

"It's beautiful," Becky gasped.

"Sure is," Cousin Verna agreed as she hopped off the wagon and pushed up her sleeves, apparently ready to plunge into the business of settling in.

They guided the cumbersome wagon carefully down into the hollow, trying to get as near to their little cabin as possible.

"All right, you youngins," Cousin Verna directed, "your pa and I will lift the heaviest things off the wagon. It's up to you to carry all your belongin's into the house. Remember now, we have only one room, so some of these crates must go up to the loft for now."

"Take care, y'hear!" Pa cautioned. "There's nothing in this here wagon that we can do without. I don't want anything to break."

Joshua and Becky were every bit as aware as their pa of their precious cargo. Why, not only were most of these things useful, but they also carried memories and traditions connected to life back east. There was Ma's spinning wheel, which Becky would now have to learn to use; clothes made especially for the first winter; furniture that could not be replaced; and much more.

With everyone eagerly helping, the wagon was unloaded in no time. Soon Cousin Verna was building a fire in the hearth and readying the kitchen for their very first meal.

*August 17: Our farm is beginning to feel more and more like our home. It seems as if we've been living here forever.*

There were more than enough chores to keep all five of them busy. Each of them worked the land every morning and then turned to other jobs.

Becky and Cousin Verna planted late summer vegetables in the kitchen garden. Mr. Benedict taught the children how to make daub by mixing a mess of dirt and straw with water. The mixture was used to repair the cracks between the logs of their cabin. Pa repaired several leaky spots in the roof.

One day Pa just up and announced that it was time they owned some animals. The next thing Joshua and Becky knew, he was pulling up beside the barn with a wagon load of sheep, plus a sow and eight little piglets.

Mr. Benedict was becoming part of the Carpenter family. Everyone liked him, especially Cousin Verna. Becky and Joshua noticed how they stared at each other in the fields and occasionally wandered off for a stroll by the creek.

Joshua thought of him as sort of an uncle. He showed up when the cock crowed at dawn every single day and stayed way past supper. Sometimes he even slept there in a makeshift bedroom he had fashioned in the Carpenters' Conestoga wagon.

While the family worked the fields, Mr. Benedict, who seemed to love the land very much, taught them new farming techniques, entertained Becky and Joshua with tales of prairie life, and warned them of some of the dangers they had to learn to expect.

One perfect summer day—not too hot, not too cold—Cousin Verna was singing as she dug her hoe in and out of the loose earth; Becky was following behind picking out all the small stones, and Pa and Joshua had just finished turning over their fourth row of soil. There seemed to be a deadly calm in the air.

Suddenly the sky went from bright blue to dark black. Within minutes, the gentle breezes they had been enjoying changed to strong winds that swirled around them, blowing specks of dirt into their eyes, taking the hats off their heads. Becky was thrown off balance and fell to the ground.

"Must be a tornado!" Pa said, looking toward the sky for the ferocious funnel that accompanied the winds. "There it is, children," he shouted, pointing to the west, his voice barely audible over the howling storm.

"Into the barn," he ordered, grabbing Becky and Joshua by the hands. Together they all pushed against the pressure, Pa pulling with all his might, as if he were dragging the oxen. When the four of them got to the barn, he yelled, "Joshua, help me shut these doors! Verna, Becky, bury yourselves under that there hay pile."

Joshua and his father braced their bodies against the closed doors as the storm came nearer and nearer. They could feel the doors shake as the wind passed over them. Five minutes later, all was still.

Pa opened the door a crack and peaked out. Miraculously, their farm was still intact. As quickly as the twister hit, it was gone.

*August 29: The tornado passing over us seemed like a good omen. Life on our farm is becoming calmer and happier. We are accomplishing so much, and the weather continues to cooperate with the crops.*

A daily rhythm began to take hold. Mornings were spent in the fields, while afternoons took on a variety of activities. Some days Cousin Verna instructed Joshua and Becky in reading and writing. Other days Joshua went off fishing with a new friend from a nearby farm. The children helped with lighter tasks such as churning butter, feeding and chasing the chickens, and making tool handles for the metal blades Pa had brought from the east.

Best of all, as September was nearing, it became obvious that there just might be a healthy harvest and the Carpenters would have food for the winter.

*September 5: Becky and I weren't much surprised by the news that Mr. Benedict sprang on us today.*

Mr. Benedict had seemed preoccupied for most of that morning, wandering around the farm and keeping pretty much to himself. After the noon meal, he uncharacteristically sat down and gazed out the window, doing absolutely nothing.

"Well, I'll be," Pa exclaimed. "I never thought I'd live to see the day when George Benedict would sit idle. You feeling all right?"

"As a matter of fact, Samuel, I'm feeling plumb perfect." A smile briefly crossed his face. "But I have been meaning to ask you something—in private, that is."

"Sure thing," Pa answered, his curiosity piqued. "I'm heading down to the wheat fields. Why don't we go together?"

They hadn't taken more than thirty paces when Mr. Benedict began. "Verna and I . . ." He hesitated, almost stuttered. "Verna and I would like to marry."

"Marry! Why, George, that's just about the best news I've been party to for a long time," Pa exclaimed, patting his friend on the back. "When's the special day?"

"Well, that's the problem," Mr. Benedict continued. "We have no house to live in, and we were wonderin' if we could stay on here until we found a place."

"I think that's a right good idea, George," Pa said. "We've grown accustomed to havin' both of you around, and to tell you the truth I can't quite imagine our farm without you."

    "That's mighty kind of you to think that
way, Samuel."
    "Then it's settled," Pa said. "We'd best get to
planning a wedding." And with that, Pa went
out back to give Verna a big hug.

*September 25: Today's the big day!*

The next few weeks went by in one dizzying blur. Once the wedding date had been set, Cousin Verna went over to Oak Grove to buy some fancy fabric for a new dress. Uncle Isaac had just gotten in some bonnets, and his niece chose a fancy yellow straw hat that framed her face when she tied it under her chin with a bright pink satin bow.

Meanwhile, Mr. Benedict took Henry and went off in search of a parson. An itinerant preacher came through Oak Grove about once a month. Mr. Benedict hoped he could find him and have him perform the wedding ceremony.

Aunt Ida wasted no time and invited all the neighbors when they came by the General Store. She had no trouble finding ladies who were eager to cook up their special party treats.

Finally the day arrived. As soon as the dew began to rise from the cool earth, guests started to trickle down the path. Everyone gathered around the bride and groom as the itinerant minister began the ceremony. Cousin Verna smiled the entire time as the preacher talked and read from the Good Book. Mr. Benedict looked fidgety, relaxing only when the preacher said, "Now let me introduce you to Mr. and Mrs. George Benedict!"

Within minutes, the parson removed his hat, took out his fiddle, and began to play. All the guests grabbed a partner, and the dancing was under way, with George and Cousin Verna leading off.

While everyone else danced, Pa just stood by and watched. Then a pretty lady walked up to him and started talking. At first Pa seemed shy, but soon Joshua could tell his father was enjoying her company. That made Joshua smile. He took hold of Becky's hand and started dancing himself.

As the music continued and the merriment increased, Joshua began to feel a tinge of happiness. The Carpenters certainly had their sad times and everything hadn't turned out as they had planned, but things sure were looking up. Ma had taught them how to meet a crisis and then go forward. As Joshua gazed around at their new home and new friends, he felt good about what they had accomplished. The Carpenters were ready to begin again—even Pa.